21st Century Skills Library

REAL WORLD MATH: PERSONAL FINANCE

USING CREDIT WISELY

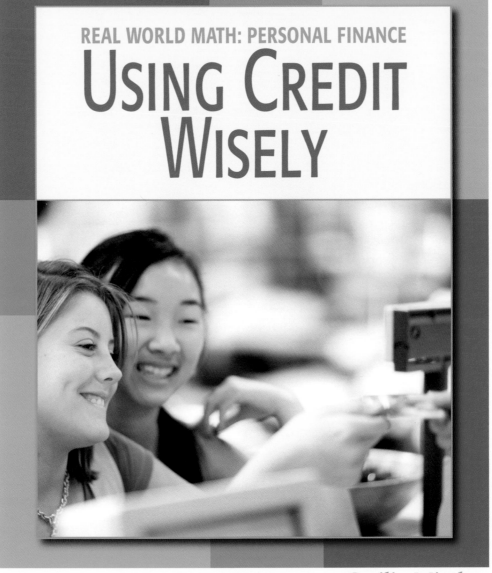

Cecilia Minden

Cherry Lake Publishing
Ann Arbor, Michigan

CHERRY
LAKE
Publishing

Published in the United States of America by Cherry Lake Publishing
Ann Arbor, MI
www.cherrylakepublishing.com

Math Education Adviser: Timothy J. Whiteford, PhD, Associate Professor of Education,
St. Michael's College, Colchester, Vermont

Finance Adviser: Ryan Spaude, CFP®, Kitchenmaster Financial Services, LLC, North
Mankato, Minnesota

Photo Credits: Cover and page 1, © Kevin Dodge/Corbis; page 4, © Najlah Feanny/
Corbis; page 17, © Joe McBride/Corbis; page 20, © James Leynse/Corbis; page 22, © Jose
Luis Pelaez, Inc./Corbis; page 28, © Paul Barton/Corbis

Library of Congress Cataloging-in-Publication Data
Minden, Cecilia.
  Using credit wisely / by Cecilia Minden.
    p. cm. — (Real world math)
  ISBN-13: 978-1-60279-002-5 (hardcover)
  ISBN-10: 1-60279-002-7 (hardcover)
  1. Consumer credit—Juvenile literature. 2. Credit—Juvenile literature. 3. Consumer credit—
United States—Juvenile literature. 4. Credit—United States—Juvenile literature. I. Title. II. Series.
  HG3755.M54 2008
  332.7'43—dc22   2007006481

Cherry Lake Publishing would like to acknowledge the work of
The Partnership for 21st Century Skills.
Please visit www.21stcenturyskills.org for more information.

TABLE OF CONTENTS

CHAPTER ONE

What Is Credit?   4

CHAPTER TWO

Kinds of Credit   8

CHAPTER THREE

Do the Math: Using a Credit Card   13

CHAPTER FOUR

Do the Math: Installment Loans   17

CHAPTER FIVE

Being Smart about Credit   21

Real World Math Challenge Answers   29

Glossary   30

For More Information   31

Index   32

About the Author   32

WHAT IS CREDIT?

Many people use credit to buy expensive items such as a new computer.

Javier wants to buy a new computer. He doesn't have enough money. His big brother Luis offers to buy a computer for him. Luis said Javier can pay back the money over three months. "You also have to wash my car every weekend," Luis adds. Javier agrees to the terms of the loan. Luis is the *lender.* Javier is the *borrower.* Javier is using credit to get his computer. The amount Javier borrows is called the principal.

When you buy something on credit, you are having someone else give you the money to pay for your purchase. The lender is taking a risk. He or she is counting on you to pay back everything that you owe. The lender wants an additional payment for taking this risk. For Luis, this additional payment is having Javier wash his car.

Unlike Luis, banks aren't going to ask you to wash cars! Instead, they are going to charge you interest. Interest is an additional amount of money added to the loan. It is a percentage of the money you have borrowed. Each month, you make a payment on the loan. This payment pays back part of the principal plus interest. You pay interest only on the principal you still owe.

Think carefully and weigh all of your options before deciding to take out a loan. You may end up paying much more than the cost of the item. For example, Keisha borrows $100,000 at 6 percent interest to buy a house. Like many home loans, her loan lasts 30 years. By the time the loan is completely paid off, Keisha will have paid the bank $215,838. The total interest was more than the amount she originally borrowed!

Every time you borrow money, it is reported to a credit bureau. Credit bureaus are businesses that create credit reports on everyone who makes payments to pay off debts. If you pay your credit card bills and other loan payments on time, you get a good credit rating. If you do not make your payments on time, you get a bad credit rating. A bad credit rating makes it difficult for you to get other loans.

Banks and other companies that are thinking about loaning you money will check your credit rating. If you have a good credit rating, they know they can trust you. They may loan you a larger amount of money.

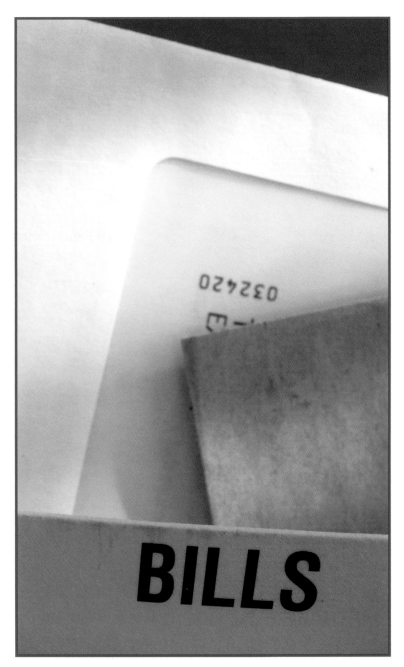

It is important to pay credit card bills and other loans on time to maintain a good credit rating.

CHAPTER TWO

KINDS OF CREDIT

Some stores that sell appliances offer installment loans to their customers.

Chad and Dara need a new refrigerator. They go to a department store and pick one out that costs $1,249.89, including tax. They don't want to pay the entire amount right away. They would rather use credit. They have two choices: use a credit card or get an installment loan.

Credit cards are issued through banks. You see people use credit cards all the time. At the checkout counter, either the cashier or the buyer will swipe the credit card through a machine. This machine confirms that the credit card is valid. Then the buyer signs a receipt and is done. No money changes hands.

When you charge something on a credit card, you are asking the bank to pay for what you bought. Once a month, you will get a bill that lists all the purchases you made on your credit card. If you pay the bill in full, the bank will not charge interest. If you pay only a portion of the total, you will be charged interest on the unpaid portion. The amount that you still owe is called the balance. Until you pay off the balance in full, you will be charged interest each month.

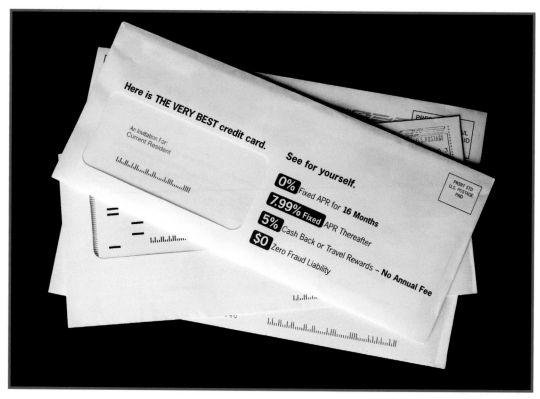

Credit card companies often send credit card offers
in the mail to try to get new customers.

When you are issued a credit card, the bank will tell you your credit

limit. That is the total amount of money you can owe on the card at any

time. Young people often have a low limit, such as $500.00. People with a

good credit history may have a limit of $10,000 or more.

What if Chad and Dara don't want to use a credit card to buy their refrigerator? They can apply for an installment loan. In an installment loan, the lender gives the borrower cash for that one purchase. The borrower uses the money to pay for the item. The borrower then pays the lender in monthly payments that include interest. Installment loans are usually for major purchases such as cars, appliances, and home repairs.

REAL WORLD MATH CHALLENGE

Jessie went shopping at the mall. She found a dress and shoes to wear to her high school graduation that's coming up in two weeks. They cost a total of $135.48. At a different store, she bought her father a pair of sunglasses for Father's Day that cost $19.99. She also bought some art supplies for a school project that cost $13.47 and three CDs at $16.97 each. She paid for everything with her credit card. **How much did Jessie charge that day?**

Jessie's family is going on vacation the day after graduation. She wants to buy a camera for the trip. She picked one out on the Internet that costs $279.00 plus $7.95 shipping. Jessie's credit card has a $500.00 limit. **Can she buy the camera with her credit card?**

(Turn to page 29 for the answers)

REAL WORLD MATH CHALLENGE

Javier used an installment loan to buy his computer. Luis was the lender. Javier's computer costs $378.00, including tax. He had $87.00 in savings. Luis agreed to loan him the rest of the money, if Javier agreed to pay it back in equal installments over the next three months. **How much did Javier borrow from Luis? How much were his monthly payments?**

Instead of washing Luis's car as interest, Javier agreed to pay 3 percent interest each month on the balance of his loan. **How much did Javier pay in interest the first month? After his first payment, what was the balance of his loan? How much interest did Javier pay the second month? The third month?** Hint: Javier paid interest only on the *balance* of the loan—that is, the amount he still owed Luis that month.

What was the total amount of interest Javier paid on the loan?

(Turn to page 29 for the answers)

The biggest expense most people have in their lifetime is buying a home. A loan to buy a home is called a mortgage. Payments on mortgages can be thousands of dollars a month. Many mortgages last for 30 years! It is too early for you to apply for a mortgage, but it isn't too early to get into the habit of paying off loans promptly. You need a good credit history to get the best rate on your mortgage.

CHAPTER THREE

DO THE MATH:
USING A CREDIT CARD

*Having a wallet full of credit cards can tempt you
to buy things that you really can't afford.*

Credit cards can be useful when we need something right away but do

not have the money to pay for it. But credit cards are a big responsibility.

With a credit card in your pocket, there is a temptation to buy whatever

you want whenever you want it. You have to remember that every time you

Don't forget that when you buy something with a credit card you will have to pay for it when the bill arrives!

charge something, you are asking the bank to buy it for you. You eventually

have to pay the bank back!

Credit cards can work for you. You can use them to establish a good

credit history. To do this, make regular payments in a timely manner.

The best plan is to pay off the balance every month, to avoid paying any

interest charges.

REAL WORLD MATH CHALLENGE

Patrick wants to buy a new mountain bike. The one he wants costs $449.99 plus 7 percent sales tax. **What is the cost of the bike?**

Patrick earns $40 a week at his part-time job. **If he saves 50 percent of his earnings each week, how long will it take for him to have enough money for the bike?**

He could have the bike right away if he uses a credit card. The credit card company will charge 18 percent annual interest on the balance. Below is a table showing his credit card payments and balances if he purchases the bike.

MONTH	BALANCE	INTEREST 18% annual	PAYMENT	REMAINDER
1	$481.49	$7.22	$80.00 ($20 x 4 weeks)	$408.71
2	$408.71	$6.13	$80.00	$334.84
3	$334.84	$5.02	$80.00	$259.86
4	$259.86	$3.90	$80.00	$183.76
5	$183.76	$2.76	$80.00	$106.52
6	$106.52	$1.60	$80.00	$28.12
7	$28.12	$0.42	$28.54	0

How long will it take Patrick to pay off his credit card, assuming he doesn't use the card for anything else?

How much interest would Patrick pay if he bought the bike with his credit card?

(Turn to page 29 for the answers)

You have to be 18 years old to apply for your own credit card. If you're younger than that, you need your parents' permission to have one. Most credit cards for high school or college students have low limits, only a few hundred dollars. Some banks also issue special prepaid credit cards for young people. Your parents transfer money out of their checking account onto the prepaid credit card. You then use it just like a regular credit card, but everything you buy has already been paid for. Prepaid credit cards allow young people to learn how to use a credit card wisely. But there is no danger that they will spend more than they can afford.

Credit cards can help you establish a good credit history if you use them responsibly.

CHAPTER FOUR

Do the Math:
Installment Loans

*Using a credit card can make it easy to buy
things you want but don't really need.*

What if you need something that costs lots of money? You know it will take

a long time to pay it off. If you use a credit card, you will be charged a high

interest rate. The average interest rate for credit cards is about 19 percent.

Instead of paying such a high rate, you might want to apply for an

installment loan. The interest on an installment loan is lower than on a

credit card because you will be making payments for a longer time.

Interest rates can change every day. They vary from bank to bank. If

you are about to make a big purchase, shop around to find the best interest

Many people use installment loans to buy new or used cars.

rate. Banks compete with one another for customers. If you have a good

credit rating, they will want you as a customer and you may be able to get

a better rate.

REAL WORLD MATH CHALLENGE

Sunny needs to buy a new car. She found a good car that she likes. She has some money saved, but she needs a $9,000 loan to pay off the car. She can get a 3-year or a 5-year loan. The 3-year loan charges 6.88 percent interest. The 5-year loan charges 6.97 percent.

Help Sunny decide which is the better choice. The loan officer gave her this information:

- $9,000 borrowed at 6.88 percent for 3 years (36 months) = $277.40 monthly car payment, including interest
- $9,000 borrowed at 6.97 percent for 5 years (60 months) = $178.08 monthly car payment, including interest

What will Sunny's total payments be if she uses the 3-year loan? How much of that is for interest?

What will Sunny's total payments be if she uses the 5-year loan? How much of that is for interest?

How much more will Sunny pay in interest with the 5-year loan?

The bank managers offer a lower payment on the 5-year loan because they know they will be getting more interest from the borrower.

(Turn to page 29 for the answers)

If you use an installment loan, you may be given an amortization schedule. An amortization schedule is a table showing how long it will take you to pay off your debt. It lists your payment each month for the duration of the loan. Then it shows how much of each payment goes to paying off the principal and how much is for interest.

You should shop around to find the bank with the best interest rate before you take out an installment loan.

BEING SMART ABOUT CREDIT

*Credit cards are convenient and can give you a
way to keep track of what you spend.*

Credit cards are a convenient way to pay for purchases. They come in

handy if you want to buy an item but don't have enough money saved up

or if you have unexpected expenses. A credit card can also be a way to keep track of expenses. Paying off a credit card promptly is a great way to build

up a good credit rating.

Make sure you check your credit card bill carefully each month and then pay it in full if you can.

Always keep in mind that credit cards charge a relatively high interest rate. Unless you pay off the card in full every month, you will have to pay interest.

When you get your credit card bill, it will list a minimum

*Make sure you read the credit card agreement carefully so
you understand all of the terms of the agreement.*

required payment. This is the lowest amount that you can pay. If you pay only the minimum, however, your balance will hardly go down, and you will end up paying a lot of interest. Let's say you have $1,000 on a credit card that charges 18 percent interest. You decide to stop using the credit card, but each month you pay only the minimum amount required. By

If you only pay the minimum amount required on your credit card bill each month, you may end up paying thousands of dollars in interest!

paying only a typical minimum payment, it will take you eight years to pay off the credit card—and by then, you will have paid $1,000 in interest. If you pay only the minimum, you will still be paying for clothes long after you've outgrown them or for a skateboard long after you've stopped using it!

Having a credit card means being responsible for keeping good records. Each time you pay for an item with your credit card, you get a receipt. Keep all of your receipts in one place. An envelope with the month written on it works well. At the end of the month, you'll receive a credit card bill showing all of your charges. Check your receipts against the charges. If they don't match up, contact the credit card company. Pay off the balance every month so you do not have to pay interest charges. If you can't do that, then pay as much as you can. Even double or triple the minimum required payment helps keep the balance low.

The average American adult has between 5 and 10 credit cards. But 1

credit card will take care of your needs. (If adults really thought about it,

most would come to the conclusion that they don't need more than 1 or 2

Most people really don't need more than 1 or 2 credit cards.

If you find that credit cards lead you to spend more than you can afford, cutting them up is a good idea!

Your credit report is often considered a reflection of your general reliability and responsibility. Rental agencies use credit reports to decide if they will let you rent an apartment. They check to see if you are sometimes late with payments and how much total debt you have. If you have a good credit rating, they trust that you will pay the rent on time and take good care of the apartment.

Many companies also check the credit ratings of people applying for jobs. If your credit report shows a big debt and many late payments, companies might think you are not responsible. They may think that you would be late to work a lot or might not finish your work on time.

either.) If you have more than 1 card, you're likely to charge more than you can afford. Once you start carrying a balance on your credit card, it can be very hard to pay off.

Keep your debts small. Pay them off in a timely manner. This is the best way to let others know you are financially responsible. It will also help keep your credit score high. Your credit report belongs to you—you own it. Make it work for you.

Credit cards are a good financial tool if they are used wisely.

REAL WORLD MATH CHALLENGE ANSWERS

Chapter Two

Page 11

Jessie spent $219.85 at the mall.

$135.48 + $19.99 + $13.47 + ($16.97 × 3) = $219.85

The total cost of the camera is $286.96. The camera plus Jessie's previous charges total $506.80. That is more than her credit limit. She cannot buy the camera with her credit card.

$279.00 + $7.95 = $286.95

$219.85 + $286.95 = $506.80

Page 12

Javier borrows $291.00 from Luis.

$378.00 − $87.00 = $291.00

Javier will pay Luis $97.00 each month.

$291.00 ÷ 3 = $97.00

Javier pays $8.73 in interest the first month.

3% of $291.00 = 0.03 × $291.00 = $8.73

Javier's balance after his first payment is $194.00.

$291.00 − $97.00 = $194.00

Javier pays $5.82 in interest the second month. After his second payment, he still owes Luis $97.00.

The third month, Javier pays $2.91 in interest.

3% of $194.00 = 0.03 × $194.00 = $5.82

$194.00 − $97.00 = $97.00

3% of $97.00 = 0.03 × $97.00 = $2.91

Javier pays a total of $17.46 in interest.

$8.73 + $5.82 + $2.91 = $17.46

Chapter Three

Page 15

The sales tax on the bike is $31.50. The bike's total cost is $481.49.

7% of $449.99 = 0.07 × $449.99 = $31.50

$449.99 + $31.50 = $481.49

Patrick can save $20.00 a week. It will take him slightly more than 24 weeks, or about six months, to save up for the bike.

50% of $40.00 = 0.50 × $40.00 = $20.00

$481.49 ÷ $20.00 = 24.07

If he paid for the bike with a credit card, it would take him seven months to pay for the bike. He would pay $27.05 in interest.

$7.22 + $6.13 + $5.02 + $3.90 + $2.76 + $1.60 + $0.42 = $27.05

Chapter Four

Page 19

With the 3-year loan, Sunny's car payments will total $9,986.40. She will pay $986.40 in interest.

$277.40 × 36 = $9,986.40

$9,986.40 − $9,000.00 = $986.40

With the 5-year loan, Sunny's total car payments will be $10,684.80. She will pay $1,684.80 in interest.

$178.08 × 60 = $10,684.80

$10,684.80 − $9,000.00 = $1,684.80

Sunny would pay $698.40 more interest with the 5-year loan.

$1,684.80 − $986.40 = $698.40

Glossary

amortization schedule (aa-mur-tuh-ZAY-shun SKE-jool) a chart that shows monthly loan payments and how much is left to be paid on a loan

balance (BA-lunts) the amount left unpaid on a credit card or loan

credit (KREH-dit) the provision of money, goods, or services with the expectation of future payment

installment loan (in-STAWL-munt LONE) a loan paid back in monthly payments

interest (IN-trust) a charge for borrowing money, usually a percentage of the amount borrowed

loan officer (LONE AW-fuh-sur) a person in charge of reviewing and granting loans

mortgage (MOR-gij) a loan to buy a house or business

principal (PRIN-suh-puhl) the unpaid balance on a loan

FOR MORE INFORMATION

Books

Harmon, Hollis Page. *Money Sense for Kids.* Hauppauge, NY: Barron's, 2004.

Heckman, Philip. *Saving Money (How Economics Works).* Minneapolis: Lerner, 2006.

Holyoke, Nancy. *A Smart Girl's Guide to Money: How to Make It, Save It, and Spend It.* Middleton, WI: American Girl, 2006.

Mayr, Diane. *The Everything Kids' Money Book: From Saving to Spending to Investing—Learn All about Money!* Cincinnati: Adams Media, 2000.

Web Sites

Moneyopolis: Where Money Sense Rules!
www.moneyopolis.org/new/home.asp
Play a game that will help teach you how to manage money

Planet Orange
www.orangekids.com/
Choose a guide and travel around Planet Orange to learn about smart money management

Young Investor
www.younginvestor.com/
Information and games to help you learn about managing money

INDEX

amortization schedules, 20

balances, 9, 12, 15, 16, 24, 25
banks, 5, 6, 9, 10, 14, 16, 18–19
bills, 6, 7, 9, 22, 24, 25
borrowers, 5, 11

credit bureaus, 6, 7
credit cards, 8, 9–10, 11, 13–14, 15, 16, 17, 21–22, 24–27
credit history, 10, 12, 16
credit limits, 10, 16
credit ratings, 6, 19, 22, 27, 28

credit reports, 6, 7, 27, 28

Fair Isaacs & Company (FICO), 7
FICO scores, 7

installment loans, 8, 11, 12, 18, 19, 20
interest, 5, 6, 9, 11, 12, 15, 16, 17, 18–19, 20, 22, 24, 25

lenders, 5, 11, 12
loans, 4–5, 6, 8, 11, 12, 18, 19

minimum payments, 22, 24–25

mortgages, 12

payments, 5, 6, 7, 11, 12, 15, 16, 18, 19, 20, 22, 24–25, 27, 28
prepaid credit cards, 16
principal, 5, 20

receipts, 25
risk, 5, 7

savings, 15

ABOUT THE AUTHOR

Cecilia Minden, PhD, is a literacy consultant and the author of many books for children. She is the former director of the Language and Literacy Program at Harvard Graduate School of Education in Cambridge, Massachusetts. She would like to thank fifth-grade math teacher Beth Rottinghaus for her help with the Real World Math Challenges. Cecilia lives with her family in North Carolina.